MASTER LUMA AI AND CREATE CAPTIVATING CONTENTS IN MINUTES

I0466753

STEPHEN HUGHES JACOBS

**Master Luma AI and Create Captivating Content in Minutes:
Table of Contents**

Chapter 1: Welcome to the World of Luma AI

- 1.1 What is Luma AI and Why Should You Care?
- 1.2 Unveiling the Power of AI-Powered Content Creation
- 1.3 Getting Started with Luma AI: A Beginner's Roadmap

Chapter 2: Demystifying the Luma AI Interface

- 2.1 A Guided Tour: Exploring the Essential Features
- 2.2 Uploading and Managing Your Media Assets
- 2.3 Customizing Your Workspace for Maximum Efficiency

Chapter 3: Mastering the Basics of Luma AI

- 3.1 The Magic of Importing: Seamlessly Integrate Your Footage
- 3.2 Editing Essentials: Trimming, Cutting, and Arranging Your Content
- 3.3 Adding Text and Overlays: Enhance Clarity and Visual Appeal

Chapter 4: Unlocking the Power of Luma AI Effects

- 4.1 Special Effects Galore: Explore Luma AI's Built-in Effects Library
- 4.2 Creating Transitions that Flow: Seamlessly Connect Your Scenes
- 4.3 Fine-Tuning Your Edits: Utilizing Advanced Effects Controls

Chapter 5: The Art of Storytelling with Luma AI

- 5.1 Crafting a Compelling Narrative: Structure and Pacing for Impact

- 5.2 Engaging Your Audience: Techniques for Capturing Attention
- 5.3 Adding Emotional Impact: Using Music and Sound Design Effectively

Chapter 6: Level Up Your Content with AI-Powered Enhancements

- 6.1 Unleashing the Magic of Auto-Reframe: Effortless Composition Adjustment
- 6.2 Background Removal Simplified: Isolate Your Subject with Ease
- 6.3 AI-powered Noise Reduction: Achieve Crisp and Professional Audio

Chapter 7: Optimizing for Different Platforms

- 7.1 Understanding Social Media Requirements: Tailoring Your Content for Success
- 7.2 Beyond the Basics: Optimizing for Audience Engagement
- 7.3 Exporting Your Masterpiece: Choosing the Right Format and Settings

Chapter 8: Advanced Techniques for Power Users

- 8.1 Working with Green Screens: Creating Stunning Chroma Key Effects
- 8.2 Customizing Motion Graphics: Add a Professional Touch with Templates
- 8.3 Leveraging Third-Party Integrations: Expand Your Luma AI Workflow

Chapter 9: The Future of Content Creation with Luma AI

- 9.1 Exploring Cutting-Edge AI Features: A Glimpse of What's to Come

- 9.2 Staying Ahead of the Curve: Resources and Tips for Continuous Learning
- 9.3 The Ethical Use of AI in Content Creation: Responsible Practices

Chapter 10: Monetizing Your Luma AI Skills

- 10.1 Building a Portfolio that Stands Out: Showcase Your Expertise
- 10.2 Finding Your Niche Specialize and Attract Targeted Clients
- 10.3 Building a Sustainable Career: Strategies for Long-Term Success

Chapter 1: Welcome to the World of Luma AI

This chapter serves as your launchpad into the exciting realm of Luma AI. Here, we'll unveil the potential of this revolutionary tool and equip you with the knowledge to become a captivating content creator in minutes.

Luma AI: Your Gateway to Effortless Content Creation

Unveiling the magic behind Luma AI: We'll delve into what Luma AI is and how it utilizes artificial intelligence to streamline the content creation process.

Why Luma AI is a game-changer: Discover the key benefits of using Luma AI, from accelerated editing to enhanced creativity.

Who can benefit from Luma AI: Explore how Luma AI empowers creators of all levels, from beginners to seasoned professionals.

The Power of AI in Content Creation

Demystifying AI-powered tools: Understand the core functionalities of AI in content creation and how Luma AI leverages them.

Traditional editing vs. AI-assisted editing: We'll compare the limitations of traditional methods with the advantages of AI-powered editing.

The future of content creation with AI: Get a glimpse of the exciting possibilities that AI holds for the future of content creation.

Getting Started with Luma AI: A Beginner's Roadmap

Setting up your Luma AI account: Navigate the initial steps of creating your account and familiarizing yourself with the platform.

Exploring the user interface: We'll take you on a guided tour of the Luma AI interface, highlighting key features and functionalities.

Your first steps in Luma AI: Learn the essential actions for importing media, creating a basic project, and exporting your final masterpiece.

1.1 What is Luma AI and Why Should You Care?

Have you ever dreamt of creating stunning video content but felt discouraged by the time commitment or technical complexities of traditional editing software? Well, fret no more! Luma AI is here to revolutionize the way you approach content creation.

Luma AI Explained:

Effortless Editing: Imagine a platform that takes the grunt work out of editing. Luma AI utilizes artificial intelligence (AI) to automate tedious tasks, allowing you to focus on the creative aspects of storytelling.

AI-Powered Enhancements: Forget spending hours on background removal or noise reduction. Luma AI's AI features handle these tasks with ease, saving you precious time and effort.

Seamless Integration: No matter if you're a seasoned videographer or a social media enthusiast, Luma AI integrates effortlessly with your existing workflow. Import your footage, add your creative touch, and export a polished product – all within minutes.

Why Luma AI Matters:

Time is Money: In today's fast-paced world, time is a valuable commodity. Luma AI helps you create captivating content efficiently, freeing up your time for other priorities.

Level Up Your Game: Whether you're a business owner, a social media influencer, or simply passionate about creating, Luma AI empowers you to produce professional-looking content that stands out.

Embrace the Future: Luma AI positions you at the forefront of content creation. By harnessing the power of AI, you'll be well-equipped to succeed in the ever-evolving digital landscape.

So, if you're ready to ditch the editing headaches and unlock a world of creative possibilities, then Luma AI is the perfect partner for you. Let's dive deeper and explore the revolutionary features that await!

1.2 Unveiling the Power of AI-Powered Content Creation

The world of content creation has undergone a significant shift with the introduction of AI-powered tools like Luma AI. Let's peel back the layers and understand how AI transforms the editing process:

AI - Your Intelligent Assistant: Imagine having a virtual assistant by your side, anticipating your needs and automating repetitive tasks. Luma AI utilizes AI algorithms to analyze your footage, suggest edits, and even apply basic effects, freeing you to focus on the bigger picture.

Goodbye Mundanity, Hello Creativity: Traditional editing software often involves tedious tasks like trimming clips, adding transitions, or adjusting audio levels. AI takes care of these mundane activities, allowing you to dedicate your energy to the creative aspects like storyboarding, adding graphics, and crafting a compelling narrative.

Smarter Editing Decisions: Luma AI doesn't just automate tasks; it can also analyze your content and suggest improvements. AI algorithms can identify areas for enhancement, such as unnecessary pauses or weak pacing, empowering you to make informed editing decisions.

The Edge Over Traditional Editing:

Speed and Efficiency: AI streamlines the editing process, allowing you to create high-quality content in a fraction of the time compared to traditional methods.

Accessibility for All: Luma AI's intuitive interface and AI-powered features make professional-grade editing accessible to creators of all skill levels, from beginners to seasoned editors.

Constant Innovation: The world of AI is constantly evolving. Luma AI leverages this ongoing development to integrate cutting-edge features and stay at the forefront of content creation technology.

A Glimpse into the Future:

AI-powered content creation is still in its nascent stages, but the potential is vast. As AI continues to develop, we can expect even more intelligent tools that can not only edit but also actively participate in the creative process, collaborating with creators to produce truly groundbreaking content.

By embracing AI-powered tools like Luma AI, you're not just simplifying your workflow; you're positioning yourself at the forefront of a content creation revolution.

1.3 Getting Started with Luma AI: A Beginner's Roadmap

Congratulations on taking the first step towards mastering Luma AI! This section will equip you with the essential knowledge to navigate the platform and embark on your content creation journey. Here's your beginner's roadmap:

Setting Up Your Account:

Signing Up Made Easy: We'll guide you through the simple signup process, whether you choose to create an account with your email address or utilize social media login options.

Navigating the Interface: Get acquainted with the Luma AI interface layout. We'll identify key elements like the project workspace, media library, and editing tools.

Customizing Your Workspace: Discover how to personalize your Luma AI experience by adjusting settings and preferences to suit your workflow.

Your First Luma AI Project:

Importing Your Assets: Learn how to seamlessly import your existing photos, videos, and audio into your Luma AI project.

Creating a Basic Project: We'll walk you through the steps of establishing a new project in Luma AI, setting the video parameters, and adding your media files.

Essential Editing Techniques: Master the fundamental editing tools within Luma AI, including cutting clips, rearranging sequences, and adding basic transitions.

Exporting Your Masterpiece:

Choosing the Right Format: Understand the different video export formats available in Luma AI and select the optimal one based on your intended platform (e.g., YouTube, social media).

Customizing Export Settings: Learn how to adjust export settings such as video resolution and bitrate to achieve the desired quality and file size balance.

Sharing Your Creation with the World: Discover how to effortlessly export your final video project from Luma AI and share it with your audience across various platforms.

By following these steps and exploring the intuitive interface of Luma AI, you'll be well on your way to creating captivating content in no time. Remember, practice makes perfect! The more you experiment and explore, the more comfortable you'll become with the vast potential of Luma AI.

Chapter 2: Demystifying the Luma AI Interface

Feeling overwhelmed by unfamiliar buttons and menus? Don't worry! This chapter will guide you through the Luma AI interface, transforming it from a mystery into a familiar and empowering tool.

2.1 A Guided Tour: Exploring the Essential Features

Feeling intimidated by the Luma AI interface? Fear not! This section is your roadmap to navigating the key areas and transforming them into powerful tools for your creative vision.

Demystifying the Workspace:

The Editing Timeline: This central stage of Luma AI is where your story unfolds. We'll break down the timeline's functionalities, allowing you to precisely arrange your clips, add transitions, and control the flow of your content.

The Preview Window: Consider this your window into the final product. Learn how to utilize the preview window to monitor your edits in real-time, ensuring your creative vision translates flawlessly.

The Media Library: This is your treasure trove of creative assets. We'll guide you through exploring and managing your imported photos, videos, and audio files within the media library.

The Effects Panel: Unleash the power of Luma AI's effects! This section houses a vast collection of tools, from basic transitions and text overlays to advanced AI-powered enhancements.

Understanding the Tools:

Editing Essentials: Master the fundamental tools within the timeline, like cutting clips, trimming unwanted footage, and duplicating segments for seamless storytelling.

Precision Editing Tools: Dive deeper and explore advanced editing functionalities like split edits, ripple edits, and slip edits to achieve professional-grade precision in your content.

Navigation and Selection: Learn how to efficiently navigate the timeline, select multiple clips, and manipulate elements within your project with ease.

Customizing Your View:

Workspace Layouts: Discover the flexibility of Luma AI's workspace layouts. Learn how to switch between different layouts to optimize the interface for specific editing tasks.

Docking and Undocking Panels: Maximize your screen real estate by strategically docking and undocking panels like the media library and effects panel based on your workflow needs.

Personalizing Your Experience: Unlock the hidden potential of Luma AI by exploring features like keyboard shortcuts and custom toolbars to personalize your editing experience.

By conquering these initial steps, you'll be well on your way to wielding the Luma AI interface with confidence. The next chapter will delve into the art of media management, ensuring your creative assets are organized and readily available for your content creation journey.

2.2 Uploading and Managing Your Media Assets: Building Your Creative Arsenal

Luma AI thrives on your creative vision, but that vision relies on having your photos, videos, and audio files readily available. This section equips you with the knowledge to effortlessly upload and manage your media assets, transforming them into a well-organized arsenal for captivating content creation.

Importing Made Simple:

Drag-and-Drop Magic: Experience the ease of importing your media. Learn how to simply drag and drop your files directly from your computer folders into the Luma AI workspace.

File Browser Navigation: For those who prefer a more traditional approach, we'll guide you through navigating your computer's file system using Luma AI's built-in file browser to locate and import your desired media.

Cloud Integration Power: Luma AI understands the convenience of cloud storage. Discover how to integrate your favorite cloud storage services like Dropbox or Google Drive to seamlessly import media files directly from the cloud.

Media Library Mastery:

The Heart of Your Project: Consider the media library your central hub for all your imported creative assets. We'll explore its functionalities, allowing you to browse, preview, and select your photos, videos, and audio files with ease.

Organization is Key: Maintaining a well-organized media library is crucial for efficient editing. Learn effective techniques for categorizing your assets using folders, tags, and custom naming conventions.

Search and Filter Efficiency: No more wasting time searching through a cluttered media library. Master the art of using Luma AI's search and filter functions to locate specific files based on name, type, or even creation date.

Essential File Management:

Keeping Things Tidy: Luma AI empowers you to keep your project workspace clean and organized. Discover how to delete unnecessary media files, rename them for clarity, and utilize version control features to track changes and revert if needed.

Project Backup Essentials: Safeguard your creative efforts! We'll guide you through establishing a solid project backup routine, ensuring your work is protected against accidental deletion or hardware failures.

Collaboration Made Easy: (Optional, if applicable to Luma AI) If Luma AI allows collaboration, this section can cover functionalities for sharing media assets with team members and managing access permissions.

By mastering these skills, you'll transform your media library from a disorganized mess to a well-oiled machine. This will allow you to focus on the creative aspects of storytelling, knowing your assets are readily available and efficiently organized for seamless content creation.

2.3 Customizing Your Workspace for Maximum Efficiency: Craft Your Luma AI Command Center

Welcome to the nerve center of your creative vision! In this section, we'll transform the default Luma AI interface into a personalized workspace tailored for maximum efficiency and streamlined editing.

Tailoring the Interface to Your Needs:

Workspace Layouts Unveiled: Luma AI offers a variety of pre-configured workspace layouts. We'll explore the functionalities of each layout, such as the editing-focused layout or the effects-oriented layout, allowing you to choose the one that best suits your current project and editing style.

Docking and Undocking for Flexibility: Master the art of docking and undocking interface panels. Learn how to strategically arrange elements like the media library, effects panel, and timeline to optimize your screen real estate and prioritize the tools you need most during specific editing tasks.

Shortcut Savvy: Keyboard shortcuts are a time-saving superpower in any editing software. We'll unveil a list of essential Luma AI keyboard shortcuts and guide you through customizing them to match your preferences and existing editing habits.

Boosting Your Productivity:

Project Templates for a Quick Start: Don't waste time reinventing the wheel! Discover how to utilize Luma AI's project templates to establish a consistent workflow and basic structure for different content types, like social media videos or explainer videos.

Batch Editing Power: For repetitive tasks, leverage the magic of batch editing. Learn how to apply edits like color correction or noise reduction to multiple clips simultaneously, saving you precious time and effort.

Auto-Save: Your Safety Net: Accidents happen, but your creative work doesn't have to suffer. Explore Luma AI's auto-save functionality and configure it to save your project at regular intervals, ensuring peace of mind and protection against unexpected software crashes.

Staying Organized:

Timeline Mastery: The editing timeline is the canvas where your story comes to life. We'll delve into advanced timeline organization techniques, such as color-coding clips for easy identification, adding markers for specific moments, and utilizing grouping functions to manage complex projects.

Commenting for Clarity: Communication is key, especially when collaborating with others. Learn how to add comments directly within the timeline to provide notes, instructions, or feedback for yourself or your team members.

Custom Workspaces for Different Projects: Take your personalization a step further! Explore the possibility of creating custom workspaces with specific layouts, tool configurations, and shortcut sets tailored for different project types, maximizing your efficiency and streamlining your workflow.

By implementing these customization strategies, you'll transform the Luma AI interface from a generic workspace into a personalized command center designed to empower your creativity and accelerate your content creation process. In the next chapter, we'll delve into the core editing functionalities of Luma AI, equipping you with the skills to bring your captivating content to life.

Chapter 3: Mastering the Basics of Luma AI: Building the Foundation for Captivating Content

Now that you've navigated the Luma AI interface and organized your creative arsenal, it's time to dive into the core editing functionalities. This chapter will equip you with the essential tools to master the basics of Luma AI and start building the foundation for your captivating content.

3.1 The Magic of Importing: Seamlessly Integrate Your Footage

The journey to captivating content creation begins with gathering your creative building blocks: your photos, videos, and audio files. Luma AI offers a variety of ways to import these assets effortlessly, ensuring a smooth integration into your project.

Effortless Importing Methods:

Drag-and-Drop Simplicity: Experience the intuitive magic of drag-and-drop. Simply locate your desired media files on your computer, then drag and drop them directly onto the Luma AI workspace. This is the quickest way to import your photos, videos, and audio for immediate editing.

File Browser Navigation: For those who prefer a traditional approach, Luma AI's built-in file browser is here to assist. Navigate your computer's file system with ease, locate specific media files using folders and filters, and import them directly into your project with a click.

Cloud Integration Power: Luma AI leverages the convenience of cloud storage. If you utilize cloud storage services like Dropbox or Google Drive, you can seamlessly import your media files directly from the cloud. This eliminates the need to download files beforehand and streamlines your workflow, especially if you work with remote teams or access your projects from different devices.

Importing Beyond the Basics:

Understanding File Compatibility: Not all file formats are created equal. While Luma AI supports a wide range of popular video and audio formats (MP4, MOV, AVI, MP3, etc.), it's always a good practice to check the software's documentation for a comprehensive list. This ensures compatibility and avoids potential issues during the editing process.

Importing for Optimal Editing: A few key considerations can significantly enhance your editing experience. Importing media with the same frame rate and resolution throughout your project helps maintain consistency and simplifies editing. Luma AI might also offer options to adjust these settings during import, so explore those functionalities if needed.

Advanced Import Options (Optional): If Luma AI offers advanced import features like batch importing or sequence importing, this section can delve deeper into their functionalities. Batch importing allows you to import multiple files simultaneously, saving time, while sequence importing can be useful for handling image sequences captured from cameras.

By mastering these importing techniques, you'll establish a smooth workflow from the very beginning of your creative process. In the next section, we'll explore the essential editing tools within Luma AI, empowering you to arrange your footage and craft a captivating narrative.

3.2 Editing Essentials: Trimming, Cutting, and Arranging Your Content

The editing timeline in Luma AI is your command center for crafting a compelling narrative. Here, you'll master the fundamental editing tools that form the backbone of captivating content creation: trimming, cutting, and arranging your media.

Taming the Footage: Trimming with Precision

Not all footage is perfect. There might be unwanted sections at the beginning or end of a clip that disrupt the flow of your story. Here's where trimming comes in:

Identifying Areas to Trim: Develop a critical eye. Watch your clips and identify any unnecessary pauses, silent intros/outros, or shaky camera movements that can be removed for a tighter edit.

The Trimming Tools: Luma AI provides user-friendly trimming tools. Locate the playhead on the timeline at the desired in-point or out-point of your clip. Drag the playhead inwards to trim the beginning or outwards to trim the end, achieving a precise and focused edit.

Advanced Trimming Techniques:

Split Trimming for Audio Independence (Optional): If Luma AI offers split trimming, explore this feature. It allows you to adjust the audio and video components of a clip separately within the timeline. This is useful for situations where you might want to trim the video but keep the original audio duration.

Cutting with Confidence: Separation and Control

Cutting allows you to divide your clips into distinct segments, providing more granular control over your narrative. Here's how to master cuts in Luma AI:

The Cutting Tool: The cutting tool acts like a scalpel for your video. Position the playhead on the timeline at the precise point where you want to make a cut. Utilize the cutting tool to slice the clip into two separate segments.

Types of Cuts: Luma AI might offer different cutting options. Explore the functionalities of basic cuts, razor blade cuts (for clean transitions between scenes), and ripple cuts (which maintain the overall edit duration by automatically adjusting nearby clips).

Beyond the Basic Cut:

Overlapping Clips for Creative Transitions (Optional): Experiment with overlapping clips on the timeline. This can create smooth visual transitions between scenes or add a dynamic effect to your content.

Arranging Your Story: Building Cohesion

Once your clips are prepped, it's time to assemble them into a cohesive sequence that tells your story:

Drag-and-Drop Sequencing: The beauty of Luma AI's timeline lies in its intuitive drag-and-drop functionality. Simply drag and drop your trimmed clips onto the timeline in the desired order to build your narrative sequence.

Reordering for Impact: Don't be afraid to experiment! Play with the order of your clips to find the sequence that best conveys your message and keeps your audience engaged.

Timeline Management Techniques: As your project grows, explore Luma AI's timeline management features. Utilize techniques like color-coding clips for easy identification or adding markers to highlight specific sections for future reference.

By mastering these editing essentials, you'll gain complete control over the structure and flow of your content. The next chapter will delve into the world of Luma AI effects, empowering you to add visual flair and elevate your creations to the next level.

3.3 Adding Text and Overlays: Elevate Your Content with Visual Storytelling

Text overlays and graphic elements are powerful tools within Luma AI's arsenal. They can transform your videos from simple footage to visually engaging content that informs, educates, or entertains your audience.

Text Overlays: Making Your Message Clear

Creating Text Overlays: Adding text overlays is a breeze in Luma AI. Locate the text overlay function within the interface (it might be a button or menu option). Click on it to create a new text element on your timeline.

Customizing Your Text: Luma AI provides a variety of options to personalize your text overlays. Explore functionalities like font selection, text size and color adjustments, and text positioning to create overlays that complement your visual style.

Animations and Motion Graphics (Optional): If Luma AI offers text animation or motion graphics presets, consider incorporating them. This can add dynamism and visual interest to your text overlays, grabbing your audience's attention and enhancing the impact of your message.

Beyond Basic Text Overlays:

Crafting Titles and Intros: Use text overlays to design impactful titles and intros that set the stage for your content. Titles should be clear, concise, and visually appealing, while intros can introduce your brand or topic in a creative way.

Lower Thirds for Key Information: Utilize lower thirds to display essential information during your video, such as names, locations, or dates. By positioning them strategically at the bottom third of the frame, you can ensure they are clear and unobtrusive.

Unveiling the Power of Overlays (Optional)

If Luma AI offers additional overlay functionalities, delve into these options to explore their creative potential:

Shape Overlays: Shapes can be used for various purposes, such as highlighting specific areas of your video, creating call-to-action buttons, or adding decorative elements. Explore different shapes and experiment with their fill colors and opacity to achieve the desired visual effect.

Image Overlays: Incorporate image overlays to showcase logos, product images, or other visuals that complement your content. Explore options for blending modes and opacity adjustments to seamlessly integrate these overlays with your video footage.

Remember:

Balance is Key: While text overlays and graphic elements can enhance your content, it's crucial to maintain a visual balance. Avoid cluttering your video with too many elements, as this can overwhelm your audience and distract from your message.

Cohesive Visual Style: Strive for a consistent visual style throughout your project. Choose fonts, colors, and graphic elements that complement each other and create a unified aesthetic for your content.

By mastering these techniques, you'll transform text and overlays from mere decorations into powerful storytelling tools within Luma AI. The next chapter will introduce you to the exciting world of effects, empowering you to add professional polish and elevate your content to new heights.

Chapter 4: Unlocking the Power of Luma AI Effects: Transforming Your Content with Creativity

Welcome to the realm of creative possibilities! This chapter unveils the magic of Luma AI effects, transforming your basic edits into visually stunning and engaging content.

4.1 Exploring the Effects Panel: Your Gateway to Creative Enhancement

The effects panel in Luma AI is your secret weapon, a treasure chest overflowing with creative tools. Mastering this section will empower you to transform your basic edits into visually stunning and captivating content.

Locating the Effects Powerhouse:

The effects panel's location can vary slightly depending on your Luma AI version. It might be a dedicated panel on the side of the workspace, conveniently docked for easy access. Alternatively, it could be nestled within a menu option readily available at your fingertips.

A Universe of Effects Awaits:

Once you locate the effects panel, prepare to be dazzled! Here, you'll discover a vast collection of effects categorized for intuitive exploration. Dive into these categories to unlock the creative potential Luma AI offers:

Transitions: These effects bridge the gap between your clips, ensuring a smooth and polished flow throughout your video.

Explore classic dissolves, energetic wipes, or stylish slides to create seamless transitions that enhance your narrative.

Understanding Effect Categories (Optional):

Motion Graphics: Breathe life into your content with dynamic elements! This category might house animated titles, social media icons, or pre-made animations that add visual interest and grab your audience's attention.

Color Correction and Grading: Take complete control over the visual aesthetics of your footage. Utilize color correction tools to fine-tune brightness, contrast, and color balance for a polished look. Feeling adventurous? Explore advanced color grading options to achieve a cinematic style that elevates your content.

Visual Effects (Optional): If Luma AI offers visual effects (VFX), this section holds the key to unlocking advanced creative possibilities. You might find tools for green screen compositing, which allows you to seamlessly replace a green background with another image or video. Object removal tools can help eliminate unwanted elements from your footage, while special effects like slow motion or time-lapse can add dramatic flair to your storytelling.

By familiarizing yourself with these effect categories, you'll be well-equipped to navigate the vast creative potential within Luma AI. The next section will delve into applying these effects with precision, transforming your basic edits into visually captivating masterpieces.

4.2 Applying Effects with Precision: Adding Visual Flair

The effects panel in Luma AI is brimming with creative potential, but applying them effectively is what truly elevates your content. This section equips you with the knowledge to add visual flair with precision, transforming your edits into polished and engaging masterpieces.

Effortless Effect Application:

Luma AI simplifies the process of incorporating effects into your project. In many instances, the application process is as easy as drag-and-drop. Simply locate the desired effect within the effects panel and drag it directly onto your clip positioned on the timeline.

Fine-Tuning the Effect (Optional):

Most effects come with adjustable parameters, allowing you to customize their impact on your video. Explore these options to achieve the specific visual outcome you desire. Here are some common parameters you might encounter:

Effect Intensity: Control the potency of the effect. Adjust the intensity slider to achieve a subtle or dramatic impact, depending on your creative vision.

Effect Duration: Define how long the effect lasts within your clip. Shorten or lengthen the duration to ensure a seamless transition or create a more extended visual flourish.

Specific Effect Properties: Depending on the effect, you might encounter additional properties for fine-tuning. For example, a color correction effect might allow adjustments to specific color ranges, while a blur effect might offer a radius control to define the intensity of the blur.

Advanced Effect Techniques (Optional):

Effect Stacking for Richer Compositions: Experiment with layering multiple effects for a more complex and visually striking outcome. Combine a color correction effect with a subtle vignette to create a vintage film aesthetic. Remember, maintain a balance – too many effects can overwhelm your viewers.

Keyframe Editing for Nuanced Control (Optional): If Luma AI offers keyframe editing, this powerful tool allows for precise control over an effect's parameters throughout the clip. You can set keyframes at specific points in the timeline and define the desired effect values at those points. This is beneficial for creating nuanced and visually captivating effects, such as a color shift that gradually transitions throughout a scene.

By mastering these application techniques, you'll gain creative control over the visual language of your content. The next section will delve into the exciting world of Luma AI's artificial intelligence, exploring features that can further enhance your editing experience.

4.3 AI-Powered Enhancements: Unleashing Luma AI's Intelligence

One of the defining features of Luma AI is its integration of artificial intelligence, designed to streamline your editing workflow and elevate the quality of your content. Here's how to leverage these AI-powered functionalities to your creative advantage:

Effortless Improvements with Automatic Enhancements (Optional): Let Luma AI's intelligence do the heavy lifting! Explore features like automatic color correction or noise reduction. With a single click, these AI-powered tools can significantly improve the overall quality of your footage, saving you time and effort while delivering professional-looking results.

AI-Generated Content for Streamlined Creation (Optional): Some versions of Luma AI might offer even more advanced AI features that can expedite your creative process. Imagine generating royalty-free background music that perfectly complements the mood and tone of your video content, or creating intros and outros with AI-powered text animation – all within Luma

AI. These features can be a game-changer for creators who want to produce high-quality content efficiently.

Beyond the Click of a Button:

Understanding AI Limitations: It's important to remember that AI-powered features are still under development. While they can be incredibly useful tools, they might not always achieve perfect results. Always review the AI-generated content and adjust it if needed to ensure it aligns with your creative vision.

Human Creativity Still Reigns Supreme: Luma AI's AI features are there to assist you, not replace your creative input. Use them as a starting point for your creativity, but don't be afraid to experiment, add your own personal touch, and make the final decisions to achieve the unique style you desire for your content.

By incorporating Luma AI's artificial intelligence features thoughtfully, you'll enhance your editing workflow and create content that looks professional and polished. The next chapter will guide you through the final stages of refining your project, prepping it for the world to see.

Chapter 5: The Art of Storytelling with Luma AI: From Editing to Captivating Content

Congratulations! You've mastered the essential tools and effects within Luma AI. Now it's time to refine your project and transform your edits into a compelling story that engages your audience.

5.1 The Power of Narrative: Crafting a Cohesive Story

At its core, every successful video is a story waiting to be told. A clear narrative provides direction for your editing choices and ensures your viewers walk away with a lasting impression. Here's how to craft a compelling story with Luma AI:

Unearthing Your Message: Before diving into the editing suite, take a moment to identify the heart of your story. What is the central message you want to convey? A well-defined message acts as a compass, guiding your creative decisions and ensuring your audience grasps the core takeaway.

Structuring Your Journey: A well-structured narrative is the backbone of audience engagement. Explore different storytelling structures to find the one that best suits your content. The classic three-act structure (beginning, middle, end) is a reliable framework, but there's room for creativity. Consider alternative structures like problem-solution, question-and-answer, or journey-based narratives depending on your story's unique flow.

Bringing Your Story to Life in Luma AI:

Sequencing with Intention: Remember those editing techniques you mastered? Now it's time to put them into action! Utilize sequencing to strategically arrange your clips in a way that unfolds your story in a logical and engaging manner. Order your edits to build suspense, reveal key moments strategically, and ensure a clear flow of information.

The Art of Pacing: Pacing refers to the speed at which you deliver your content. Varying the pace throughout your video is essential for keeping your audience hooked. Fast-paced cuts can create excitement and urgency, while slower sections allow viewers to absorb information and connect with the emotional core of your story.

By mastering these fundamental storytelling concepts, you'll lay the groundwork for transforming your edits into a captivating narrative. The next section will delve into the finishing touches that elevate your project to a professional level.

5.2 Adding Polish and Professionalism: The Finishing Touches

The final editing stages are where your project truly transforms from a collection of edits into a polished and professional piece of content ready to captivate your audience. Luma AI provides a variety of tools to add that extra layer of refinement.

Elevating Your Audio: The Power of Sound

High-quality audio is an often-underestimated aspect of professional video production. Luckily, Luma AI offers features to enhance the sonic landscape of your project:

Audio Editing for Clarity: Utilize Luma AI's audio editing tools to adjust volume levels and ensure a balanced soundscape. You can eliminate background noise, remove unwanted audio sections, or fade in/out music and sound effects to create smooth transitions.

Enhancing the Mood with Music and Sound Effects: Music and sound effects are powerful storytelling tools. Luma AI might offer a built-in library or allow you to import your own audio assets. Explore these options to add background music that complements the mood and tone of your video, or incorporate sound effects to emphasize specific actions or create a sense of immersion for your viewers.

Adding Visual Polish:

Text Overlays and Titles that Shine: Refine your text overlays and titles for optimal impact. Ensure they are clear, concise, and visually appealing by adjusting font size, color, and positioning. Consider adding subtle animations or effects to titles to create a touch of dynamism and grab your audience's attention.

Final Touches and Considerations:

Exporting for Different Platforms: Luma AI likely offers various export options tailored for specific platforms. These options might include presets for common resolutions and frame rates optimized for YouTube, social media sharing, or website embedding. Choose the appropriate export format to ensure your video looks its best on the platforms where you plan to share it.

Calls to Action (Optional): A strong call to action (CTA) tells your audience what you want them to do after watching your video. This could be anything from subscribing to your channel to visiting your website or learning more about your product or service. Consider adding a clear and concise CTA at the end of your video to leave a lasting impression and prompt viewers to take action.

By incorporating these finishing touches, you'll transform your project from a basic edit into a professional-looking video that stands out from the crowd. The next section will delve into some advanced storytelling techniques you can explore to truly push the boundaries of creative video editing with Luma AI.

5.3 Beyond the Basics: Exploring Advanced Storytelling Techniques with Luma AI

Luma AI empowers you to go beyond basic editing and tell stories in unique and captivating ways. Here are some advanced techniques to elevate your video editing skills and create content that truly wows your audience:

Visual Storytelling with Motion Graphics and Overlays:

Leveraging Motion Graphics: Move beyond static text overlays. Explore Luma AI's motion graphics capabilities (if available) to create dynamic and visually engaging elements. Animated titles, intros, social media icons, or even lower thirds with subtle animations can significantly enhance your storytelling and capture attention.

Illustrative Overlays for Impact: Consider incorporating illustrative overlays or infographic elements to explain complex concepts in a visually engaging way. Luma AI might allow you to import vector graphics or create basic shapes to complement your narrative and add visual interest.

Using Transitions for Mood and Flow:

Transitions are more than just a way to connect clips. Strategic use of transitions can significantly impact the mood, pacing, and overall flow of your story:

Creative Transitions for Different Effects: Experiment with different transition types beyond the basic cuts and dissolves. Luma AI might offer wipes, slides, pushes, or even more artistic transitions. Choose transitions that complement the mood you want to create, whether it's a smooth and polished flow, a fast-paced and energetic feel, or a classic cinematic style.

Transitions for Emotional Impact: Don't underestimate the power of transitions to evoke emotions. A slow, dissolving transition between scenes can create a sense of nostalgia or dreaminess, while a quick cut with a jarring sound effect can surprise your viewers and add a sense of urgency.

Remember:

Storytelling is a Journey: Developing strong storytelling skills takes time and practice. Analyze successful videos in your niche, experiment with different techniques in Luma AI, and don't be afraid to iterate and refine your approach with each project.

Embrace the Power of Luma AI: Luma AI is your creative partner in storytelling. Utilize the tools and functionalities explored in this guide to push the boundaries of your creativity and craft content that resonates with your audience on a deeper level.

By mastering these advanced techniques and staying true to your unique storytelling voice, you'll be well on your way to creating professional-looking videos that capture attention, engage your audience, and leave a lasting impression. Congratulations on embarking on this exciting journey of video storytelling with Luma AI!

Chapter 6: Level Up Your Content with AI-Powered Enhancements: Unleashing Luma AI's Creative Potential

Luma AI stands out from the crowd with its integration of artificial intelligence, designed to streamline your workflow and elevate the quality of your video content. This chapter delves into the exciting realm of AI-powered features within Luma AI, empowering you to:

- **Effortlessly Enhance Your Footage (Optional):**
- **Generate Creative Assets to Expedite Production**
- **Navigate the Nuances of AI for Optimal Results**

6.1 Effortless Enhancements for a Polished Look (Optional)

Let Luma AI's intelligence do the legwork for you! Explore features like automatic enhancements to save you time and ensure a polished look for your video content:

One-Click Color Correction: Breathe new life into your footage with AI-powered color correction. In a single click, Luma AI can analyze your clips and adjust brightness, contrast, and color balance for a balanced and visually pleasing aesthetic. This is particularly helpful for beginners or when you're working with a large volume of footage and need a quick way to achieve a consistent look throughout your video.

Intelligent Noise Reduction for Crisp Clarity: Eliminate unwanted grain or video noise that can detract from your content's professionalism. AI-powered noise reduction can significantly improve the overall quality of your footage, especially for videos shot in low-light conditions or with older cameras.

Remember: While AI enhancements are incredibly useful time-savers, they might not always achieve perfect results for every situation. Here are some additional considerations:

Review and Refine: It's always recommended to preview the adjustments made by the AI, especially for color correction. You might find that the automatic settings don't quite match your creative vision or the specific lighting conditions in your footage. Luma AI should allow you to fine-tune the color correction parameters manually to achieve the desired look.

Fine-Tuning for Artistic Control: For more advanced color correction, you might prefer to use Luma AI's manual color correction tools. This gives you greater creative control over the final look of your video, allowing you to achieve specific color grading effects or match the color palettes of other video elements.

By understanding the capabilities and limitations of AI enhancements, you can leverage them effectively to streamline your workflow and achieve a polished look for your video content. The next section will delve into AI-powered creative asset generation, another exciting feature that can expedite your video production process.

6.2 Generate Creative Assets to Expedite Production (Optional)

AI-Powered Content Creation: Streamlining Your Workflow

Luma AI takes video editing a step further by offering AI-powered content generation, allowing you to create essential video elements directly within the software. This can significantly reduce production time and open doors for creative exploration. Here are some of the potential features you might encounter:

AI-Generated Music for the Perfect Mood (Optional):

Imagine having access to a vast library of royalty-free background music that perfectly complements the mood and tone of your video content, all without ever leaving Luma AI. Some versions might offer AI-powered music generation. You can specify the desired mood (upbeat, melancholic, energetic) and receive unique music tracks that seamlessly integrate with your video. This eliminates the need to search for external music libraries or commission composers, saving you valuable time and resources.

Exploring the Power of AI Music Generation (Optional):

Customization Options: Look for features that allow you to further customize the AI-generated music. You might be able to adjust the length, tempo, or instrumentation to perfectly match the specific needs of your video.

Genre and Style Selection: Some AI music generation tools might offer a variety of genre and style options, allowing you to choose from a wide range of possibilities to suit the theme and tone of your content.

AI-Powered Intros and Outros for a Professional Touch (Optional):

Crafting intros and outros can be a time-consuming process. Luma AI might offer AI-powered intro and outro generation, allowing you to streamline this aspect of your workflow. Here's how it might work:

Effortless Intro and Outro Creation: Simply input your text and branding preferences. The AI will then generate visually appealing title sequences and closing animations, complete with text animation and subtle effects. This can save you a significant amount of time and effort compared to creating these elements from scratch.

Maintaining Creative Control Over AI-Generated Assets (Optional):

While AI-generated content offers a great starting point, it's important to maintain creative control over the final product:

Customization and Refinement: Don't hesitate to customize the generated music or intros/outros to align perfectly with your unique style and branding. You might be able to adjust the text fonts, colors, or animation styles within Luma AI to achieve the desired look and feel.

Human Creativity Still Reigns Supreme: AI should be seen as a valuable assistant, not a replacement for your creativity. Use these features to spark ideas and expedite your workflow, but always inject your own creative touch and make final decisions based on your artistic judgment.

The Future of AI-Generated Content (Optional):

The field of AI-powered content creation is constantly evolving. Keep yourself updated on the latest developments in Luma AI's capabilities. New features might emerge, offering even more creative possibilities to generate video elements like titles, lower thirds, or even motion graphics, further streamlining your video production process.

By leveraging Luma AI's AI-powered content generation features effectively, you can create professional-looking videos in less time, allowing you to focus on the core aspects of storytelling and content creation. The next section will explore the nuances of working with AI and how to achieve optimal results.

6.3 Navigating the Nuances of AI for Optimal Results

Luma AI's AI-powered features are designed to empower you and streamline your video editing workflow. This section delves into understanding the potential limitations of AI and offers tips for achieving optimal results:

Understanding AI's Strengths and Limitations:

While AI is constantly evolving, it's important to remember that it's still under development. Here's a breakdown of what to expect:

Powerful Tool, Not a Replacement: AI features are incredibly useful for automating repetitive tasks, generating creative content ideas, and enhancing footage. However, they shouldn't replace your creative decision-making and artistic vision.

Room for Improvement: AI-generated content might not always be perfect. For example, automatic color correction might not always achieve the exact color grading you have in mind, or AI-generated music might not perfectly capture the specific emotional nuance you desire.

Tips for Working Effectively with AI in Luma AI:

Review and Refine: Always preview and assess the output of AI features before finalizing your project. Luma AI should allow you to refine and adjust the AI-generated content (e.g., color correction parameters, music edits) to ensure it aligns with your creative vision.

Maintain Creative Control: Don't be afraid to experiment and customize the AI-generated assets. Use them as a starting point and leverage your own creativity to personalize them and achieve the desired impact within your video.

Staying Ahead of the Curve:

The field of AI is constantly evolving, and Luma AI is likely to receive updates and introduce new AI-powered features over time. Here's how to stay informed:

Luma AI Updates and Documentation: Keep an eye on Luma AI's official channels for updates, announcements, and documentation related to new AI functionalities. These resources will provide valuable information on how to leverage the latest AI features and maximize their potential in your video editing workflow.

The Creative Community: Engage with the Luma AI community forums or social media groups. This is a great way to connect with other creators, share experiences with AI features, and learn from each other's creative approaches to using Luma AI's functionalities.

By understanding the capabilities and limitations of AI, combined with a critical eye and a touch of creative intervention, you can harness the power of Luma AI's intelligent features to significantly enhance your video editing experience. The next chapter will guide you through the final stages of preparing your masterpiece for the world to see!

Chapter 7: Optimizing for Different Platforms: Sharing Your Masterpiece with the World

Congratulations! You've transformed raw footage into a captivating story with Luma AI. Now it's time to share your creation with the world. This chapter explores the crucial step of optimizing your video content for different online platforms:

7.1 Understanding Platform Requirements: Tailor Your Video for Success

Every online platform has its own set of specifications and recommendations for video content. Here's how to ensure your video looks its best and reaches its target audience:

Decoding the Jargon: Before diving into specifics, let's break down some key terms you'll encounter:

File Format: This refers to the container that stores your video data. Common formats include MP4, MOV, and AVI. Think of it like a box that holds your video content.

Resolution: This refers to the number of pixels displayed horizontally and vertically, determining the overall image quality. Higher resolutions like 1080p (Full HD) and 4K (Ultra HD) offer sharper images, but also require larger file sizes.

Frame Rate: This refers to the number of images (frames) displayed per second, affecting video smoothness. Standard frame rates are 24fps (frames per second) for cinematic feel and 30fps for a smoother viewing experience.

Bitrate: This refers to the amount of data used to store video information per second. Higher bitrates result in higher quality videos, but also larger file sizes. Imagine it like the water pressure in a hose - higher bitrate means more data flows through, creating a clearer picture but using more storage space.

Researching Platform Guidelines: Now that you're familiar with the terms, it's time to research! Different platforms have specific requirements for each aspect mentioned above. Here's how to find this information:

Platform Help Centers: Most online platforms have comprehensive help centers with detailed information about video uploads. Search for terms like "video upload guidelines" or "supported video formats" on the platform's website.

Community Forums: Online communities dedicated to specific platforms can also be a valuable resource. Search for forums where creators share their experiences and troubleshoot upload issues.

Examples: Here are some common video platforms and their typical requirements:

YouTube: Generally recommends MP4 format with H.264 video codec and AAC audio codec. Resolution recommendations vary depending on content type, but commonly include 1080p (Full HD) and 1440p (Quad HD) for standard videos. Frame rate of 24fps or

30fps is common. Bitrate depends on resolution, but YouTube offers encoding presets to optimize file size and quality.

Social Media (Facebook, Instagram): These platforms prioritize fast loading times, so smaller file sizes are preferred. They often have specific video length limitations and recommend formats like MP4 with H.264 codec. Frame rate of 30fps is common. Bitrate is usually adjusted automatically during upload based on the chosen format and resolution.

Luma AI likely offers export presets tailored for popular platforms. These presets consider factors like resolution, frame rate, and bitrate to ensure your video meets the basic requirements of your chosen platform. By understanding these technical aspects and leveraging Luma AI's export options, you'll be well on your way to seamless video sharing across different online destinations.

The next section will explore how to go beyond basic optimization and truly capture your audience's attention on each platform.

7.2 Beyond the Basics: Optimizing for Audience Engagement

Optimizing for platform specifications is crucial for ensuring your video can be uploaded and played correctly. But to truly stand out and captivate viewers, you need to tailor your content for each platform's unique audience and viewing habits. Here's how to go beyond the basics and optimize for engagement:

Understanding Platform Cultures: Each platform fosters a distinct user culture. Here are some examples:

YouTube: In-depth tutorials, reviews, and gaming content thrive here. Viewers expect clear calls to action, like subscribing to your channel or visiting your website.

Social Media (Facebook, Instagram): Short, eye-catching videos with engaging captions and trending hashtags are key. Leverage these platforms for teasers, trailers, or behind-the-scenes glimpses to promote your longer content hosted elsewhere.

Niche Platforms: Highly specific content tailored to the platform's community interests is crucial. Actively engage with viewers in the comments to build relationships and a loyal following.

Content Tailoring for Different Attention Spans: Viewers have varying attention spans depending on the platform. Here's how to adapt:

YouTube: You have more creative freedom with video length on YouTube. However, grabbing viewers' attention within the first 30 seconds is crucial.

Social Media: Keep it short and sweet! Platforms like Instagram often have video time limitations. Focus on the most impactful moments or use strong visuals to hook viewers in the first few seconds.

Platform-Specific Optimization Techniques: Here are some additional tweaks to consider:

Titles and Descriptions: Craft compelling titles and descriptions that are relevant to each platform's search algorithms and user behavior. For example, hashtags might be more important for

Instagram videos compared to YouTube videos. Optimize these elements to ensure your video gets discovered by the right audience.

Captions and Subtitles: Platforms with autoplay without sound (like Facebook) might benefit from adding captions for silent videos. This allows viewers to understand the content even if they don't have the sound on.

Intros and Outros: Tailor the length and style of your intro/outro depending on the platform. Keep them snappy for social media and consider adding calls to action specific to that platform (e.g., "Follow us on Instagram").

Remember: While technical specifications are important, prioritize creating high-quality content that resonates with your target audience on each platform. Think about what value you bring to the platform's community and tailor your content accordingly.

The next section will delve into venturing beyond the mainstream and exploring video sharing on niche platforms.

7.3 Beyond the Big Players: Exploring Niche Platforms

The online video landscape extends far beyond the likes of YouTube and social media giants. Niche platforms cater to specific communities and interests, offering unique opportunities to connect with a highly engaged audience. Here's how to leverage niche platforms for video sharing and audience growth:

Finding Your Niche: The first step is identifying niche platforms that align with your content and target audience. Here are some resources to get you started:

Online Directories: Websites like "[alternativeto.net]" allow you to search for alternative video platforms based on features and categories. Explore categories relevant to your niche and discover potential platforms.

Social Media Communities: Online communities dedicated to your niche might have discussions about preferred video platforms within their community. Join relevant groups and see where fellow enthusiasts share their video content.

Understanding Niche Platform Requirements: Similar to mainstream platforms, niche platforms might have specific video format and size limitations. Here's how to ensure smooth uploads:

Platform Help Centers: Most niche platforms have help centers with detailed information about video uploads. Search for terms like "video upload guidelines" or "supported video formats" on the platform's website.

Community Forums: Niche platform communities are often tight-knit. Search for forums where creators share their experiences and ask questions about video uploads. This can provide valuable insights specific to the platform.

Building a Community on Niche Platforms: Niche platforms thrive on audience interaction and community engagement. Here are some tips to stand out:

Tailored Content: Create content that resonates deeply with the platform's specific interests. Show your passion and understanding of the niche community.

Active Participation: Don't just upload and disappear! Actively engage with viewers in the comments section, respond to questions, and participate in discussions. This fosters a sense of community and builds relationships with viewers.

Collaboration Opportunities: Niche platforms often encourage collaboration between creators. Consider partnering with other creators on video projects to expand your reach within the community.

By following these steps, you can leverage niche platforms to connect with a dedicated audience, establish yourself as a thought leader within your niche, and potentially grow your online presence beyond the mainstream.

The next chapter will explore some additional tips for promoting your video content and maximizing your reach across all platforms.

Chapter 8: Advanced Techniques for Power Users: Unleashing the Full Potential of Luma AI

Congratulations! You've mastered the fundamentals of video editing with Luma AI and are well on your way to creating professional-looking content. This chapter dives into advanced techniques designed to empower power users and push the boundaries of creative video editing.

8.1 Advanced Editing Workflows: Streamlining Your Process

As you delve deeper into video editing with Luma AI, efficiency becomes paramount. Here are some advanced techniques to streamline your workflow and maximize your editing time:

Keyboard Shortcut Mastery: Become a keyboard shortcut ninja! Luma AI likely offers a comprehensive set of keyboard shortcuts for common editing actions. Dedicating some time to learn and memorize these shortcuts can significantly accelerate your editing workflow. Look for a comprehensive list of shortcuts within Luma AI's documentation or settings menu.

Customizable Workspaces for Optimized Layouts: Luma AI might allow you to personalize your editing workspace. Organize tools, panels, and windows in a way that suits your editing style. This can significantly improve your efficiency, especially when working on complex video projects with numerous elements. Experiment with different layouts to find what works best for you.

Project Management and Organization for Clarity: For large projects with numerous video clips and audio tracks, organization is key. Utilize Luma AI's project management features (if available) to create folders, label clips clearly with descriptive names, and add color coding for easy identification. This keeps your project well-structured and simplifies navigation, saving you time searching for specific clips later.

Proxy Editing for Smoother Performance on Less Powerful Machines: When working with high-resolution footage or complex edits, your editing experience might become bogged down due to processing demands. Proxy editing allows you to edit lower-resolution versions of your clips while maintaining the full-resolution quality for final export. This ensures smoother playback and editing performance, especially on computers with less powerful graphics cards or processors.

Batch Processing for Repetitive Edits: Need to apply the same edit (like color correction or watermarking) to multiple clips? Explore Luma AI's batch processing capabilities (if available). This allows you to select multiple clips and apply the desired edit in one go, saving you valuable time and effort. Batch processing is ideal for repetitive tasks that would otherwise be time-consuming to apply individually.

By incorporating these advanced workflow techniques, you'll become a more efficient video editor with Luma AI, allowing you to focus on your creative vision and deliver high-quality content faster. The next section will explore advanced effects and transitions to elevate your storytelling to the next level.

8.2 Mastering Effects and Transitions for Captivating Storytelling

Luma AI goes beyond basic editing tools, offering a treasure trove of advanced effects and transitions to elevate your storytelling and visually captivate your audience. This section delves into techniques for power users who want to push the boundaries of creativity.

Advanced Blending Modes for Creative Transitions: Move beyond basic cuts and dissolves. Explore Luma AI's advanced blending mode options, such as multiply, lighten, or screen. These modes can create unique visual effects when transitioning between clips, adding depth, interest, and a sense of style to your storytelling. Experiment with different blending modes to see how they affect the flow and mood of your video.

Motion Tracking and Masking for Precision Effects: Want to add dynamic text overlays that follow a moving object on screen, or blur out a specific element within a clip? Luma AI's motion tracking features (if available) can track the movement of an object and attach your overlay elements, creating a professional and polished look. Similarly, masking allows you to isolate specific areas of a clip and apply effects selectively. This is perfect for highlighting key elements, adding subtle enhancements, or even creating censor bars.

Customizable Animation Presets for Dynamic Visuals: Luma AI might offer pre-built animation presets for titles, text overlays, and other elements. However, power users can often delve deeper and customize these presets to achieve unique and dynamic animations that perfectly match their creative vision. Play with animation timing, easing curves, and other parameters to create animations that are fluid, eye-catching, and enhance your video's overall style.

Green Screen Keying for Professional Compositing: Take your video productions to the next level with green screen keying. This technique allows you to replace a green background with any other video or image, creating professional-looking composite shots. This is perfect for interviews, special effects, creating fantastical environments, or even product demonstrations. Mastering green screen keying opens doors to a world of creative possibilities.

Advanced Color Grading Techniques for Mood and Atmosphere: Fine-tune the mood and atmosphere of your videos with advanced color grading techniques. Luma AI might offer color wheels, curves, and other tools to achieve specific color looks or emulate cinematic styles. You can create a vibrant and energetic feel with a warm color palette, or a suspenseful mood with cooler tones and deeper shadows. Experiment with color grading to add depth and emotional impact to your storytelling.

Remember: When it comes to effects and transitions, the key is to use them strategically and with purpose. Don't overwhelm your viewers with excessive bells and whistles. Use these tools to enhance your story, guide the audience's focus, and create a visually engaging experience. The next section will explore advanced audio editing and mixing techniques to take your video's sound design to a professional level.

8.3 Advanced Audio Editing and Mixing for a Professional Sound

Luma AI doesn't just focus on visuals. It empowers you to create a truly immersive experience by crafting a professional-sounding audio mix. This section dives into advanced audio editing and mixing techniques for power users who want to refine their productions and captivate viewers with a dynamic soundscape.

Dialogue Cleaning and Noise Reduction for Clarity: Ensure your dialogue is crisp and clear, the foundation of any engaging video. Utilize Luma AI's audio editing tools to remove unwanted background noise, clicks, pops, or hums that can detract from the listening experience. Tools like noise reduction and equalization (EQ) can significantly improve the quality of your dialogue and ensure viewers can hear every word.

Multitrack Editing and Mixing for Complex Soundscapes: For projects with multiple audio sources (e.g., dialogue, music, sound effects), Luma AI might offer multitrack audio editing capabilities. This allows you to control the volume levels, panning (placement in the stereo image), and EQ of each audio track independently. This granular control is essential for achieving a professional and balanced soundscape, where all elements blend seamlessly and complement each other.

Foley Sound Design and Sound Effects Integration for Immersion: Elevate the immersion and emotional impact of your videos with strategic sound design. Luma AI might offer a sound effects library or allow you to import your own. Carefully chosen sound effects can add realism to actions on screen, emphasize key moments, and create a more engaging soundscape. For instance, footsteps in a forest scene or a subtle whoosh when a character throws a punch can significantly enhance the viewing experience.

Audio Automation for Dynamic Mixing and Cohesive Flow: For a truly polished sound experience, explore audio automation features (if available). This allows you to automate volume and EQ adjustments over time within your project. Imagine gradually lowering background music during dialogue scenes for better clarity, or subtly increasing the bass as an action sequence unfolds. Audio automation helps create smooth transitions and dynamic changes in your audio mix that perfectly complement the visuals, keeping the audience engaged throughout.

By mastering these advanced audio editing and mixing techniques, you'll be well-equipped to create professional-looking videos that not only impress viewers visually, but also captivate them with a dynamic and immersive audio experience. The next chapter will explore essential tips for collaborating with others and maximizing the potential of Luma AI for teamwork and streamlined production workflows.

Chapter 9: The Future of Content Creation with Luma AI

Congratulations! You've reached the final chapter of this comprehensive guide to Luma AI. Throughout this journey, you've explored the software's features, learned editing techniques, and discovered how to optimize your content for various platforms. Now, let's delve into the exciting possibilities that lie ahead for content creation with Luma AI.

9.1 Artificial Intelligence: A Powerful Partner, Not a Replacement

Here's a breakdown of how AI will enhance the creative process:

Supercharged Efficiency: Imagine AI handling the mundane tasks that eat up time. Luma AI could automatically generate rough cuts, synchronize sound with video, or even balance color correction across multiple clips. This frees you up to focus on the big picture: storytelling, shot selection, and adding that special creative touch.

Smarter Content Decisions: AI is getting really good at understanding video content. In the future, Luma AI might analyze your footage and suggest optimal cut points, recommend royalty-free music that perfectly complements the mood, or even generate captions based on the dialogue. This can be a huge time-saver and a source of inspiration for those "what if" creative moments.

A Personalized Editing Experience: Luma AI has the potential to become an extension of your creative vision. The software might learn your editing style and preferences over time, suggesting relevant tools and features as you work. Imagine Luma AI anticipating your needs and streamlining your workflow for maximum efficiency.

AI is a powerful tool, but it won't replace human creativity. Instead, it will augment your skills and empower you to create content faster and more efficiently, allowing you to focus on the aspects that truly set your work apart: your unique voice and creative vision.

9.2 The Power of Collaboration: Luma AI and Teamwork

Luma AI isn't just a playground for solo creators. The future of video editing is brimming with potential for collaborative content creation, and Luma AI is perfectly positioned to be a hub for teamwork. Here's how Luma AI can revolutionize the way teams work together:

Real-Time, Cloud-Based Editing: Imagine a world where multiple editors can work on the same project simultaneously. With cloud-based Luma AI, this becomes a reality. Editors working remotely or in different studios could collaborate seamlessly, each making edits to their assigned sections of the video simultaneously. This streamlines the editing process, especially for large projects with tight deadlines.

Effortless Feedback and Approval Workflows: Forget endless email chains and version confusion! Luma AI might integrate feedback and approval systems directly within the platform. Team members could leave timestamped comments directly on clips, suggest edits, and approve or reject different versions of the project, all within the Luma AI interface. This fosters clear communication and keeps everyone on the same page.

Robust Version Control and Project Management: Collaboration necessitates keeping track of changes. Luma AI might offer comprehensive version history, allowing teams to revert to previous edits, compare different versions, and see exactly who made what changes. This ensures transparency, prevents accidental overwrites, and empowers informed decision-making throughout the editing process.

Beyond these core features, imagine the possibilities:

Shared Asset Libraries: Teams could create and share libraries of pre-approved graphics, animations, sound effects, and music clips within Luma AI. This ensures brand consistency and saves time searching for assets across different systems.

Role-Based Access Control: Luma AI might offer different user permissions, allowing editors to focus on their assigned tasks while team leads maintain control over the overall project.

By embracing these collaborative features, Luma AI can transform the way video editing teams work together. Imagine geographically dispersed teams working in real-time, streamlined feedback workflows, and a transparent edit history, all within a single platform. This future of collaborative video editing is on the horizon with Luma AI.

9.3 Embracing New Horizons: The Evolving Landscape of Content Creation with Luma AI

The landscape of content creation is constantly shifting, and Luma AI is poised to be a powerful tool at the forefront of these advancements. Here's a glimpse into the exciting possibilities that lie ahead:

Integration with Cutting-Edge Technologies: Luma AI is likely to embrace emerging technologies like virtual reality (VR) and augmented reality (AR). Imagine a future where you can create interactive VR experiences or seamlessly add AR elements to your videos, all within the familiar Luma AI interface. This opens doors for innovative storytelling techniques and immersive audience experiences.

AI-Powered Content Creation for Niche Markets: Luma AI's ability to analyze content and generate creative assets can be applied to cater to specific niches. Imagine AI creating explainer videos in specialized scientific fields, automatically translating and tailoring content for different languages and cultures, or generating content specifically targeted to local audiences. This can democratize content creation and bridge communication gaps across the globe.

Democratization of Content Creation for Everyone: With AI's assistance, creating high-quality content becomes more accessible than ever before. Luma AI has the potential to empower anyone to become a content creator, regardless of their prior editing experience. Imagine AI offering intuitive guidance, suggesting edits, and even generating basic content drafts, allowing aspiring creators to focus on their unique ideas and storytelling voice.

Here are some additional thoughts on the democratization of content creation:

Lowering the Barrier to Entry: Luma AI's user-friendly interface and AI-powered assistance can make video editing less intimidating for beginners. This can lead to a surge of new content creators and a wider variety of voices and perspectives being represented online.

Focus on Creativity Over Technical Expertise: With AI handling technical aspects like video stabilization or basic color correction, creators can spend more time on the creative side of things: crafting engaging narratives, developing their unique style, and focusing on what truly matters – their message and how they want to present it to the world.

Rise of Micro-Content Creators: The ease of use offered by Luma AI might empower creators to produce shorter, snackable content pieces that are perfect for social media platforms. This could lead to a new wave of micro-content creators who specialize in creating quick, informative, or entertaining bite-sized videos.

By staying informed about Luma AI's ongoing development and embracing these future possibilities, you'll be well-positioned to leverage the power of AI to create not just visually appealing content, but content that is truly innovative, impactful, and reaches a wider audience than ever before.

This concludes our comprehensive guide to Luma AI. We hope it has equipped you with the knowledge and skills to create professional-looking videos and become a master of your craft. Now, it's your turn to unleash your creativity and share your stories with the world!

Chapter 10: Monetizing Your Luma AI Skills

Congratulations! You've mastered the art of video editing with Luma AI and are now capable of creating high-quality content. But what if you want to turn your skills into a source of income? This chapter explores various avenues for monetizing your expertise in Luma AI video editing.

10.1 Freelancing: Offering Your Luma AI Skills to the World

The magic of Luma AI is in your fingertips, and you're ready to turn your editing expertise into a thriving freelance business. This section dives into how you can leverage your Luma AI skills to land freelance gigs and establish yourself as a sought-after video editor.

Finding Your Clients:

Freelance Marketplaces: Popular platforms like Upwork, Fiverr, or Freelancer.com are bustling marketplaces teeming with potential clients. Create a compelling profile that showcases your:

Luma AI Expertise: Highlight your proficiency in Luma AI's features and how you can utilize them to create exceptional videos.

Video Editing Experience: Showcase your past projects or create a demo reel to demonstrate your editing skills and visual style.

Target Audience: Identify your niche. Are you geared towards social media content creation, explainer videos, or corporate edits? Tailor your profile to resonate with your ideal clients.

Direct Client Outreach: Don't be shy about reaching out directly! Network with businesses, marketing agencies, YouTubers, or social media influencers who might need video editing services. Craft a captivating introduction highlighting your Luma AI skills and how you can specifically benefit their content creation process.

Niche Market Specialization: Go beyond generic editing services. Identify niche markets where Luma AI's strengths can be particularly valuable. For example:

Offer real estate video editing services for local agents, showcasing properties with smooth transitions and dynamic effects.

Specialize in creating educational videos for medical professionals, utilizing Luma AI's tools for clear and concise presentations.

Standing Out from the Crowd:

Build a Portfolio that Shines: First impressions matter! Create a portfolio website or online video channel that showcases your best work. Here's what to include:

High-Quality Video Samples: Demonstrate the breadth and depth of your editing skills with a curated selection of projects edited with Luma AI.

Variety is Key: Include videos from different genres (e.g., social media edits, explainer videos, product demonstrations) to display your versatility.

Client Testimonials (if possible): Positive feedback from satisfied clients adds credibility and social proof to your portfolio.

Competitive Rates: Research standard freelance rates for video editing in your region. Here's a pricing strategy to consider:

Start Strategically: Begin with competitive rates to attract clients and build your experience.

Gradually Increase Rates: As you gain experience, build a strong portfolio, and acquire positive client reviews, you can gradually increase your rates to reflect your growing value.

Communication is Key: Excellent communication is the cornerstone of successful client relationships. Here are some best practices:

Active Listening: Understand your client's needs and vision for the project. Ask clarifying questions to ensure you're on the same page.

Regular Updates: Keep your clients informed throughout the editing process. Provide progress updates, share drafts for feedback, and be open to revisions.

Professional Demeanor: Maintain a professional and courteous tone in all communication. Meet deadlines consistently and respond promptly to inquiries.

By following these steps and constantly honing your Luma AI skills, you'll be well-positioned to establish yourself as a top-notch freelance video editor. The next section will explore additional ways to monetize your expertise, such as selling video templates and presets.

10.2 Packaging Your Expertise: Selling Video Templates and Presets

Luma AI's power extends beyond one-off editing projects. You can transform your skills into passive income by creating and selling high-quality video templates and presets. This section explores how to turn your Luma AI mastery into reusable assets that other creators can leverage.

Finding Your Marketplace:

Luma AI Marketplace (if available): Many editing platforms offer built-in marketplaces where users can buy and sell project assets. If Luma AI has one, this is a prime location to showcase your creations:

Pre-Edited Video Templates: Create intros, outros, transitions, or lower-thirds specifically designed for Luma AI. Offer a variety of styles (e.g., corporate, energetic, educational) to cater to different needs.

Editable Luma AI Project Files: Package project files with pre-applied effects, motion graphics, color grading, and customizable placeholders. This allows buyers to easily integrate these elements into their own videos.

Third-Party Marketplaces: If Luma AI doesn't have a marketplace, explore established platforms like Envato Elements or Motion Array. These websites specialize in selling video editing assets compatible with various editing software, including Luma AI.

Crafting High-Value Assets:

Market in Demand: Identify popular video editing trends and create templates that address those needs. For instance, design templates for social media posts optimized for specific platforms like Instagram Reels or TikTok.

Professional Polish: Ensure your templates and presets are polished and professional. Here's what to consider:

High-Quality Visuals: Use royalty-free stock footage, motion graphics, and images that elevate the overall aesthetic of your templates.

Royalty-Free Sound and Music: Include copyright-cleared sound effects and background music to enhance the viewing experience without copyright concerns for your buyers.

Customizable Elements: Make your templates adaptable! Allow buyers to easily replace text, images, or videos with their own content.

Clear Descriptions and Previews: High-quality assets deserve clear communication. Here's how to effectively showcase your offerings:

Detailed Descriptions: Provide potential buyers with a comprehensive understanding of what your templates or presets include. Specify features, functionalities, and any software requirements.

Compelling Previews: Use short video previews to demonstrate how your templates and presets can be used in real-world scenarios. This will entice potential buyers and showcase the value you offer.

Remember: Building a successful marketplace business takes time and consistency. Continuously create new, high-quality assets, gather positive reviews, and stay updated on design trends to stay ahead of the curve. The next section will delve into leveraging your expertise through content creation and consulting services.

10.3 Sharing Your Knowledge: Content Creation and Consulting Services

Luma AI's capabilities extend far beyond just editing your own videos. You can use your expertise to educate and empower others, building a reputation as a Luma AI authority and generating income through content creation and consulting services. Here's how to turn your knowledge into valuable resources for aspiring video editors.

Building a Learning Community:

YouTube Channel: Establish a YouTube channel focused on Luma AI video editing tutorials. Cater to different experience levels by offering:

Beginner Tutorials: Cover the fundamentals of Luma AI, guiding viewers through the interface, basic editing techniques, and creating their first videos.

Intermediate Tutorials: Delve deeper into Luma AI's features, showcasing advanced editing techniques like motion tracking, green screen keying, and audio mixing.

Advanced Tutorials: Explore creative workflows, explore niche applications of Luma AI, and share tips and tricks for optimizing videos for specific platforms.

Luma AI Consulting: If you have in-depth knowledge of Luma AI's functionalities, consider offering consulting services. Here are some ways to help businesses and individuals:

Workflow Optimization: Assist clients in setting up efficient editing workflows within Luma AI, maximizing their productivity and time management.

Advanced Techniques Exploration: Guide clients through exploring advanced features like color grading, masking, and animation to elevate their video productions.

Troubleshooting Technical Issues: Offer support to clients who encounter technical difficulties with Luma AI, helping them identify and resolve problems.

Online Courses: Package your knowledge into comprehensive online courses hosted on platforms like Udemy, Skillshare, or even self-hosted platforms. Cater to different learning styles with:

Video Lectures: Create in-depth video tutorials that walk viewers through Luma AI's features and editing workflows step-by-step.

Downloadable Resources: Provide supplemental materials like cheat sheets, project files, or practice exercises to solidify learning.

Interactive Elements: Consider incorporating quizzes, assignments, or live Q&A sessions to boost engagement and knowledge retention.

Standing Out as an Educator:

Engaging Content: Focus on creating valuable and engaging content that educates and inspires viewers. Here are some tips:

Clear and Concise Communication: Present information in a clear, easy-to-understand manner. Use visuals, screen recordings, and demonstrations to illustrate complex concepts.

Enthusiasm is Contagious: Let your passion for video editing shine through! Your enthusiasm will make the learning process more enjoyable and motivate viewers to keep learning.

Respond to Your Audience: Actively engage with your audience members. Respond to comments, answer questions, and address their specific needs and challenges.

SEO for Visibility: Optimize your YouTube channel description, course listings, or website content with relevant keywords to improve search engine visibility. This helps potential students discover your valuable Luma AI learning resources.

Community Building: Foster a sense of community around your content creation efforts. Here are some ways to connect:

Respond to Comments: Engage in discussions, answer questions, and provide constructive feedback to build relationships with your audience.

Social Media Promotion: Promote your content on social media platforms like Twitter, Facebook, or LinkedIn groups geared towards video editing.

Live Streams or Webinars: Host live sessions where you can answer questions in real-time, showcase practical editing exercises, and interact directly with your audience.

By consistently creating high-quality content, establishing yourself as a reliable source of Luma AI knowledge, and fostering a supportive learning community, you can successfully turn your expertise into a thriving content creation or consulting business. Remember, the more you share your knowledge, the more you solidify your reputation as a Luma AI guru, attracting potential clients and students who want to learn from your experience.

www.ingramcontent.com/pod-product-compliance
Lightning Source LLC
Chambersburg PA
CBHW071957210526
45479CB00003B/975